The Relevance of the Communist Manifesto

The Relevance of the Communist Manifesto

Slavoj Žižek

polity

First published in German as *Die verspätete Aktualität des Kommunistischen Manifests* © S. Fischer Verlag GmbH, Frankfurt am Main, 2018

This English edition © Polity Press, 2019
Reprinted: 2019 (three times), 2020, 2021

Polity Press
65 Bridge Street
Cambridge CB2 1UR, UK

Polity Press
101 Station Landing
Suite 300
Medford, MA 02155, USA

ISBN-13: 978-1-5095-3610-8
ISBN-13: 978-1-5095-3611-5 (pb)

A catalogue record for this book is available from the British Library.

Library of Congress Cataloging-in-Publication Data
Names: Zizek, Slavoj, author.
Title: The relevance of the Communist manifesto / Slavoj Ziʔek.
Description: Cambridge, UK ; Medford, MA : Polity Press, [2019] | Includes
    bibliographical references and index.
Identifiers: LCCN 2018043366 (print) | LCCN 2018045327 (ebook) | ISBN
    9781509536122 (Epub) | ISBN 9781509536108 (hardback) | ISBN 9781509536115
    (pbk.)
Subjects: LCSH: Marx, Karl, 1818-1883. | Marx, Karl, 1818-1883. Manifest der
    Kommunistischen Partei. | Capitalism--Social aspects.
Classification: LCC HX39.5 (ebook) | LCC HX39.5 .Z59 2019 (print) | DDC
    335.4/22--dc23
LC record available at https://lccn.loc.gov/2018043366

Typeset in 12.5 on 15 pt Adobe Garamond by
Servis Filmsetting Ltd, Stockport, Cheshire
Printed and bound in the United States by LSC Communications

For further information on Polity, visit our website:
politybooks.com

The end is near... only not the way we imagined it

There is an exquisite old Soviet joke about radio Erevan. A listener asks: 'Is it true that Rabinovitch won a new car on lottery?' The radio answers: 'In principle yes, it's true, only it wasn't a new car but an old bicycle, and he didn't win it but it was stolen from him.' Does exactly the same not hold for *The Communist Manifesto*? Let's ask radio Erevan: 'Is this text still actual today?' We can guess the answer. In principle, yes: it describes wonderfully the mad dance of capitalist dynamics, which reached its peak only today, more than a century and a half later; but... Gerald A. Cohen enumerated the four features of the classic Marxist notion of the working class: (1) it constitutes the majority in society; (2) it produces the wealth of society; (3) it consists of the exploited members of society; (4) its members are the needy people in society. When these four features are combined, they generate two further features: (5) the working class has nothing to lose from revolution; (6) the working class can and will engage in a

I

revolutionary transformation of society.[1] None of the first four features applies to today's working class, which is why features (5) and (6) cannot be generated. (Even if some of the features continue to apply to parts of today's society, they are no longer united in singe agent: the needy people in society are no longer the workers, etc.) – Correct as it is, this enumeration should be supplemented by a systematic theoretical deduction: for Marx, they all follow from the basic position of a worker who has nothing but his labour power to sell. As such, workers are by definition exploited; with the progressive expansion of capitalism, they constitute the majority which also produces the wealth; and so on. How, then, are we to find a revolutionary perspective and redefine it in today's conditions? Is the way out of this predicament a combinatorics of multiple antagonisms, their potential overlapping? But – to use Laclau's terms – how is it possible to form a 'chain of equivalences' from classic proletarians, precariat, unemployed, refugees, oppressed sexual and ethnic groups, and the like?

1 G.A. Cohen, *If You're an Egalitarian, How Come You're So Rich?* Cambridge, MA: Harvard University Press 2001.

A good starting point here would be to follow the good old Marxist path and shift the focus from politics to the signs of postcapitalism that are discernible within global capitalism itself. And we don't have to look far: the public figures who exemplify the privatization of our commons – Elon Musk, Bill Gates, Jeff Bezos, Mark Zuckerberg, all 'socially conscious' billionaires – leave bagfuls of warnings in their trail. They stand for global capital at its most seductive and 'progressive' – in short, at its most dangerous. (In a speech to Harvard graduates in May 2017, Zuckerberg told his public: 'Our job is to create a sense of purpose!' This comes from a man who, with Facebook, has created the world's most expansive instrument of purposeless loss of time.) From Zuckerberg to Gates and Musk, they all warn that 'capitalism as we know it' is approaching its end and advocate countermeasures such as minimal income. One cannot but recall here the famous Jewish joke quoted by Freud: 'Why are you telling me you are going to Lemberg when you are really going to Lemberg?' Here a lie assumes the form of a factual truth: the two friends established an implicit code by which, when you plan to go to Lemberg, you announce that you will go to Cracow and vice versa, so that, within this space, telling the literal truth means lying. And is it not the case that exactly the same holds for Zuckerberg, Musk, and other false prophets of the end of capitalism? We should simply reply to them: 'Why are you telling us that capitalism is coming to an end when capitalism is really coming to an end?' In short, their version of the end of capitalism is the capitalist version of its own end, where everything will change so that the basic structure of domination will remain the same...

More serious is the rise of what Jeremy Rifkin calls the 'collaborative commons' (CC), a new mode of production and exchange that leaves behind private property and market exchange: in CC individuals are giving their products for free, releasing them into circulation. This emancipatory dimension of CC should, of course, be located in the context of the rise of what is called 'the internet of things' (IoT) in combination with another result of today's development of productive forces: the explosive rise of 'zero marginal costs' whereby more and more products, and not only information, can be reproduced for no additional costs. The IoT is the network of physical devices, vehicles, buildings, and other items embedded in electronics, software, sensors, actuators, and network connectivity that enable these objects to collect and exchange data; it allows objects to be sensed and controlled remotely, across an existing network infrastructure. Thus the IoT creates opportunities for a more direct integration of the physical world into computer-based systems and causes improved efficiency, accuracy, and economic benefit across the board. When the IoT is augmented with sensors and actuators, the technology becomes an instance of the more general class of cyberphysical systems, which also encompass technologies such as smart grids, smart homes, intelligent transportation, and smart cities; each thing is uniquely identifiable through its embedded computing system and is able to interoperate within the existing internet infrastructure. The interconnection of these embedded devices (including smart objects) is expected to usher in automation in nearly all fields, while also enabling advanced applications such as a smart grid and expanding to the areas such as smart cities. 'Things' can also refer to a wide variety of devices such as heart-monitoring implants, biochip transponders on farm animals, electric clams in coastal waters, automobiles with built-in sensors, and DNA analysis devices for environmental, food, or pathogen monitoring. These devices collect useful data with the help of various existing technologies and then autonomously reflow these data between other devices. Human individuals, too, are 'things' whose states and activities are continuously registered and transmitted without their knowledge: their physical movements, their financial transactions, their health, their eating and drinking habits, what they buy and sell, what they read, listen to, and watch are all collected in digital networks that know them better than they know themselves.

The prospect of the IoT seems to compel us to turn Friedrich Hölderlin's famous line '[b]ut where the danger is also grows the saving power' upside down: 'but where the saving power is also grows the danger' (*wo aber das Rettende ist, wächst die Gefahr auch*). The 'saving' aspect of the IoT was described in detail by Jeremy Rifkin, who claims that, for the first time in human history, a path of overcoming capitalism is discernible as an actual tendency in social production and exchange, namely the growth of cooperative commons, so that the end of capitalism is on the horizon. The crudest Marxist hypothesis seems to be re-vindicated: the development of new productive forces makes capitalist relations obsolete. The ultimate irony is that, while former communists (China, Vietnam) are today the best managers of capitalism, developed capitalist countries go furthest in the direction of collaborative or cooperative commons as the way to overcome capitalism.

But this gives birth to new dangers, even if we discount false worries such as the idea that IoT will boost unemployment. (Isn't this 'threat' a good reason to reorganize production so that workers will work much less? In short, isn't this 'problem' its own solution?) At the concrete level of social organization, the danger is a clearly discernible tendency of the state and private sector to regain control over the cooperative commons: personal contacts are privatized by Facebook, software by Microsoft, search by Google... To grasp these new forms of privatization, one should critically transform Marx's conceptual apparatus. As a result of his neglect of the social dimension of 'general intellect' – which is, roughly, the collective intelligence of a society – Marx didn't envisage the possibility of *privatizating general intellect itself*, but this is what lies at the core of the struggle for 'intellectual property'. Negri is right here: within this frame, exploitation in the classic Marxist sense is no longer possible – which is why it has to be enforced more and more through direct, legal measures, in other words by a noneconomic force. This is why today exploitation more and more takes on the form of rent: as Carlo Vercellone put it, postindustrial capitalism is characterized by 'the profit's becoming rent'.[2] And this also explains why direct authority is needed: it is needed to impose the arbitrary yet legal conditions for the extraction of rent, conditions that are no longer 'spontaneously' generated by the market. Perhaps therein resides the fundamental 'contradiction' of today's postmodern capitalism: while its logic is deregulatory, antistatal, nomadic–deterritorializing, and so on, the key tendency in it, that of the profit to become rent, signals the strengthening role of the state, whose (not only) regulatory function is more and more all-present. Dynamic deterritori-

2 See *Capitalismo cognitivo*, edited by Carlo Vercellone. Rome: manifestolibri 2006.

8

alization coexists with and relies on increasingly authoritarian interventions by the state and its legal and other apparatuses. What one can discern as looming on the horizon of our historical becoming is thus a society in which libertarianism and individual hedonism coexist with (and are sustained by) a complex web of regulatory state mechanisms. Far from disappearing, the state is becoming stronger today.

When, due to the crucial role of general intellect in the creation of wealth through knowledge and social cooperation, forms of wealth are more and more out of all proportion to the direct labour time spent on their production, the result is not, as Marx seems to have expected, the self-dissolution of capitalism, but the gradual and relative transformation of the profit generated through the exploitation of labour – its transformation, namely, into rent appropriated through the privatization of general intellect. Let us consider the case of Bill Gates. How did he become the richest man in the world? His wealth has nothing to do with the production costs of the products that Microsoft is selling, in fact one can even argue that Microsoft is paying its intellectual workers a relatively high salary; which means that Gates's wealth is not the result of his success either in producing better software for lower prices than his competitors or in exerting a more ruthless exploitation over his hired intellectual workers. If it were, Microsoft would have gone bankrupt long ago: people would have massively chosen programs like Linux, which are free and, according to specialists, of better quality than Microsoft. Why, then, are millions still buying Microsoft? Because Microsoft imposed itself as a quasi-universal standard that almost monopolized the field, a kind of direct embodiment of general intellect. Gates became the richest man in a couple of decades by appropriating the rent for allowing millions of intellectual workers to participate in the new form of general intellect that he privatized and controls. Is it true, then, that today's intellectual workers are no longer separated from the objective conditions of their labour (they own their laptops, for example) – which is Marx's description of capitalist alienation? Yes; but, more fundamentally, *no*: they are cut off from the social field of their work, from a general intellect that is not mediated by private capital.

What ghosts are haunting us today?

All these paradoxes of the contemporary global capitalism compel us to confront in a new way the old question of spectrality, of ghosts haunting our unique historical situation. The most famous ghost that has been roaming around in the last 150 years was not a ghost of the past, but the spectre of a revolutionary future – that, of course, of the first sentence from *The Communist Manifesto*. Today's enlightened liberal reader is bound to have an automatic reaction to the *Manifesto*. Isn't this text simply wrong, on so many empirical accounts, in the picture it gives of the social situation as well as in the revolutionary perspective it sustains and propagates? Was there ever a political manifesto that was more clearly falsified by the subsequent course of history? Isn't the *Manifesto*, at its best, an exaggerated extrapolation of certain tendencies discernible in the nineteenth century? But let us approach the *Manifesto* from the opposite end. Where do we live *today*, in our global 'post-' (postmodern, postindustrial) society? The slogan that increasingly foists itself on us is 'globalization' – the brutal imposition of a unified world market that threatens all local ethnic traditions, including the very form of nation-state. If we look at it from this perspective, is not the description of the social impact of the bourgeoisie that we find in *The Manifesto* more actual than ever?

The bourgeoisie cannot exist without constantly revolutionizing the instruments of production, and thereby the relations of production, and with them the whole relations of society. Conservation of the old modes of production in unaltered form was, on the contrary, the first condition of existence for all earlier industrial classes. Constant revolutionizing of production, uninterrupted disturbance of all social conditions, everlasting uncertainty and agitation distinguish the bourgeois epoch from all earlier ones. All fixed, fast-frozen relations, with their train of ancient and venerable prejudices and opinions, are swept away, all new-formed ones become antiquated before they can ossify. All that is solid melts into air, all that is holy is profaned, and man is at last compelled to face with sober senses his real conditions of life, and his relations with his kind. The need of a constantly expanding market for its products chases the bourgeoisie over the whole surface of the globe. It must

nestle everywhere, settle everywhere, establish con-
nexions everywhere.

The bourgeoisie has through its exploitation of
the world market given a cosmopolitan character
to production and consumption in every country.
To the great chagrin of reactionists, it has drawn
from under the feet of industry the national ground
on which it stood. All old-established national
industries have been destroyed or are daily being
destroyed. They are dislodged by new industries
whose introduction becomes a life and death question for all civilized nations, by industries that no
longer work up indigenous raw material, but raw
material drawn from the remotest zones; industries
whose products are consumed, not only at home,
but in every quarter of the globe. In place of the old
wants, satisfied by the production of the country, we
find new wants, requiring for their satisfaction the
products of distant lands and climes. In place of the
old local and national seclusion and self-sufficiency,
we have intercourse in every direction, universal
interdependence of nations. And, as in material,
so also in intellectual production. The intellectual
creations of individual nations become common
property. National one-sidedness and narrow-
mindedness become more and more impossible, and

from the numerous national and local literatures there arises a world literature.[3]

Is this not, more than ever, our reality today? Toyota cars are manufactured 60 per cent in the United States, Hollywood culture pervades the remotest parts of the globe… What is more, the same goes for all forms of ethnic and sexual identity. Should we not supplement Marx's description along these lines, adding that sexual 'one-sidedness and narrow-mindedness', too, 'become more and more impossible' and that 'all that is solid melts into air, all that is holy is profaned' also in the area of sexual practices, where capitalism tends to replace the standard normative heterosexuality with a proliferation of unstable shifting identities and orientations? Today's celebration of 'minorities' and 'marginals' *is* the predominant majority position; even alt-rightists who complain about the terror of

3 Chapter 1 in Karl Marx and Friedrich Engels, *The Communist Manifesto*, 1987–2000 [1848], translated by Samuel Moore in collaboration with Friedrich Engels [1888]. Marx/Engels Internet Archive, https://www.marxists.org/archive/marx/works/1848/communist-manifesto/ch01.htm (quoted with small amendments). All quotations from *The Manifesto* come from here.

liberal political correctness present themselves as protectors of an endangered minority. Or take the critics of patriarchy – those left-wing cultural theorists who focus their critique on patriarchal ideologies and practices: they attack them as if patriarchy were still a hegemonic position, ignoring what Marx and Engels wrote 170 years ago, in the first chapter of *The Communist Manifesto*: 'The bourgeoisie, wherever it has got the upper hand, has put an end to all feudal, *patriarchal,* idyllic relations.' Is it not the time to start wondering why patriarchal phallogocentrism was elevated into a main target of criticism at the exact historical moment – ours – when patriarchy definitely lost its hegemonic role, when it began to be progressively swept away by the market individualism of 'rights'? What becomes of patriarchal family values when a child can sue his or her parents for neglect and abuse – that is, when the family and parenthood itself are, *de iure*, reduced to a temporary and dissolvable contract between independent individuals? (Incidentally, Freud was well aware of this: for him, the decline of the Oedipal mode of socialization was the historical precondition for the rise of psychoanalysis.) This means that *the critical statement that patriarchal ideology continues to be today's hegemonic ideology* is *today's hegemonic ideology*; its function is to enable us to evade the deadlock of hedonist permissiveness, which is effectively hegemonic.

Marx himself from time to time underestimated this ability of the capitalist universe to incorporate the transgressive urge that seemed to threaten it; for example in his analysis of the American Civil War, which was still going on, he claimed that England would be forced to intervene directly to prevent the abolition of slavery, since the English textile industry, the backbone of the industrial system, could not survive without the supply of cheap cotton from the American South that only slave labour rendered possible. So yes, this global dynamism described by Marx that causes all things solid to melt into thin air is our reality – on condition that we do not forget to supplement this image from the *Manifesto* with its inherent dialectical opposite: the 'spiritualization' of the material process of production itself. While capitalism does abolish the power of the old ghosts of tradition, it generates some ghosts of its own, and monstrous ones at that. Capitalism involves a radical secularization of social life, in that it mercilessly tears apart the aura of any value such as authentic nobility, sacredness, or honour:

> It has drowned the most heavenly ecstasies of religious fervour, of chivalrous enthusiasm, of philistine senti-mentalism in the icy water of egotistical calculation. It has resolved personal worth into exchange value, and in place of the numberless indefeasible chartered freedoms has set up that single, unconscionable freedom – Free Trade. In one word, for [an] exploitation veiled by religious and political illusions, it has substituted naked, shameless, direct, brutal exploitation.[4]

At this point we reach the supreme irony of how ideology functions today: it appears precisely as its own opposite, as a radical critique of ideological utopias. The predominant ideology today is not a positive vision of some utopian future but a cynical resignation, an acceptance of how 'the world really is', accompanied by a warning that, if we want to change it (too much), only totalitarian horror can ensue. Every vision of another world is dismissed as ideology. Alain Badiou put it in a wonderful and precise way: the main function of ideological censorship today is not to crush

4 Ibid.

actual resistance – this is the job of repressive state apparatuses – but to crush hope, to denounce immediately every critical project as opening a path at the end of which lies something like a gulag. This is what Tony Blair had in mind when he recently asked: 'Is it possible to define a politics that is what I would call post-ideological?'[5] In its traditional mode, ideology uses a familiar injunction: 'You have to be stupid not to see this!' You have to be stupid not to see – what? The place will be filled by whatever ideological element is supposed to make sense of a confused situation and explain it. In anti-Semitism, for example, you have to be stupid (enough) not to see the Jew as the secret agent who pulls strings behind the scenes and controls the entire social life. Today, however, in its predominantly cynical functioning, the ruling TINA ['there is no alternative'] ideology claims the opposite: 'you have to be stupid to see this'. To see what, exactly? To see hope for a radical change.

The fundamental lesson of the 'critique of political economy' elaborated by the mature

5 Quoted from http://www.newyorker.com/culture/persons-of-interest/the-return-of-tony-blair.

Marx in the years after the *Manifesto* is that this reduction of all heavenly chimeras to brutal economic reality generates a spectrality of its own. Therein resides, at core, the epistemological break that begins with the *Grundrisse* manuscripts and finds its ultimate expression in *Capital*. Let us compare the starting point of *Capital* with the starting point of Marx's earlier view in its most detailed presentation, which occurs in the first part of *The German Ideology* (this text was written in 1845, three years before the *Manifesto*, and belongs in the same period). In what is presented as a self-evident direct reference to a 'real-life process' as opposed to ideological phantasmagorias, ahistorical ideology is reigning at its purest:

> The premises from which we begin are not arbitrary ones, not dogmas, but real premises from which abstraction can only be made in the imagination. They are the real individuals, their activity and the material conditions under which they live, both those which they find already existing and those produced by their activity. These premises can thus be verified in a purely empirical way. ... Men can be distinguished from animals by consciousness, by religion or anything else you like. They themselves begin to

distinguish themselves from animals as soon as they begin to produce their means of subsistence, a step which is conditioned by their physical organization. By producing their means of subsistence men are indirectly producing their actual material life.[6]

This materialist approach is then aggressively opposed to idealist mystification:

In direct contrast to German philosophy, which descends from heaven to earth, here we ascend from earth to heaven. That is to say, we do not set out from what men say, imagine, conceive, nor from men as narrated, thought of, imagined, conceived, in order to arrive at men in the flesh. We set out from real, active men, and on the basis of their real life process we demonstrate the development of the ideological reflexes and echoes of this life process. The phantoms formed in the human brain are also, necessarily, sublimates of their material life process, which is empirically verifiable and bound to mate-

6 Karl Marx and Friedrich Engels, *The German Ideology*, 2000 [1845]. Marx/Engels Internet Archiv, http://www.marxists.org/archive/marx/works/1845/german-ideology/ch01a.htm (quoted with small amendments; full text at https://www.marxists.org/archive/marx/works/download/Marx_The_German_Ideology.pdf).

rial premises. Morality, religion, metaphysics, all the rest of ideology and their corresponding forms of consciousness thus no longer retain the semblance of independence. They have no history, no development; but men, developing their material production and their material intercourse, alter, along with this their real existence, their thinking and the products of their thinking. Life is not determined by consciousness, but consciousness by life.[7]

This attitude culminates in a hilariously aggressive comparison: philosophy stands to the study of real life just as masturbation stands to the real sexual act… Here, however, problems begin: what Marx discovered through his problematics of commodity fetishism was a phantasmagoria or illusion that could not be simply dismissed as a secondary reflection because it was operative within the 'real production process', at its very heart. Note the first words of the subchapter on commodity fetishism in *Capital*:

A commodity appears at first sight an extremely obvious, trivial thing. But its analysis brings out that it

7 Ibid.

is a very strange thing, abounding in metaphysical subtleties and theological niceties.[8]

Marx does not claim, in the usual 'Marxist' way of *The German Ideology*, that critical analysis should demonstrate how a commodity – which appears to be a mysterious, theological entity – emerged out of the 'ordinary' real-life process; he claims, on the contrary, that the task of critical analysis is to unearth the 'metaphysical subtleties and theological niceties' of what appears to be, at first sight, just an ordinary object. Commodity fetishism – our belief that commodities are magical objects, endowed with an inherent meta-physical power – is not located in our mind, in the way we (mis)perceive reality, but in the social reality itself. (Note also the strict homology with Lacan's notion of fantasy as constitutive of every 'real' sexual act: for Lacan, our 'normal' sexual act *is* precisely an act of 'masturbation with a real partner', which is to say that, in it, we do not relate to the real other but to an other reduced to

8 Karl Marx, *Capital: Volume 1*, 1995–2015 [1867], translated by Samuel Moore and Edward Aveling [1887]. Marx/ Engels Internet Archive, http://www.marxists.org/archive/marx/ works/1867-c1/ch01.htm.

a fantasy object; we desire the other insofar as this person fits the fantasy coordinates that structure our desire.) The circle is thereby closed. If Marx started from the premise that the critique of religion is the beginning of all critique and then went on to the critique of philosophy, of state, and so on, ending with the critique of political economy, this last critique brought him back to the starting point: the 'religious'–metaphysical moment at work at the very heart of the most 'earthly' economic activity.

Fictitious capital and the return to personal domination

It is this spectral dimension, underestimated by Marx himself, that allows us to account for the historical deadlock of Marxism. The mistake of Marxism was not just that it counted on the prospect of capitalism's final crisis, and therefore could not grasp how capitalism came out of each crisis strengthened. There is a much more tragic mistake at work in the classic body of Marxism, described in precise terms by Wolfgang Streeck: Marxism was right about the 'final crisis' of capitalism, we are clearly entering it today, but this crisis is just that – a prolonged process of decay and disintegration with no easy Hegelian *Aufhebung* in sight, no agent to give this decay a positive twist and to transform it into a passage to some higher level of social organization:

> It is a Marxist – or better: modernist – prejudice that capitalism as a historical epoch will end only when a new, better society is in sight, and a revolutionary subject ready to implement it for the advancement of mankind. This presupposes a degree of political control over our common fate of which we cannot even dream after the destruction of collective agency, and indeed the hope for it, in the neoliberal–globalist revolution.[9]

Streeck enumerates different signs of this decay: lower profit rate, the rise of corruption and violence, financialization (i.e. profit from financial dealings that is parasitic upon value production). The paradox of the financial politics of the United States and European Union is that gigantic inputs of money fail to generate production,

9 Wolfgang Streeck, *How Will Capitalism End?* London: Verso Books 2016, p. 57.

since they mostly disappear in the operations of fictitious capital. This is why one should reject the standard liberal Hayekian interpretation of the exploding debt (the costs of welfare state): data clearly show that the bulk of these inputs goes to feed financial capital and its profits. Along these lines, Rebecca Carson[10] deploys how the financialization of capital – whereby most profit is generated in interest-bearing capital or money that creates money (M-M′) without a detour through the valorization of the labour force that produces surplus value – paradoxically leads to the return of direct personal relations of domination – paradoxically because, as Marx emphasized, M-M′ is capital at its most impersonal and abstract. It is crucial to grasp here the link between three elements: fictitious capital, personal domination, and the social reproduction (of labour power). Financial speculations take place before the fact (of valorization): they mostly consist of credit operations and speculative investments where no money is yet spent on investment in

10 See Rebecca Carson, 'Fictitious Capital, Personal Power and Social Reproduction', unpublished manuscript, 2017 (not paginated).

production. Credit means debt, and therefore the subjects or bearers of this operation (not just individuals, but banks and institutions that manage money) are not involved in the process only as subjects to the value form; they are also creditors and debtors, and hence subject to another form of power relation, which is not based on the abstract domination of commodification:

> Hence, the particular power relation involved in credit operations has a personal dimension of dependency (credit–debt) that is differentiated from abstract domination. This personal power relation, however, comes into being by the very process of exchange that is described abstractly by Marx as completely impersonal and formal since the social relations of credit operations are built on the social relations of the value form. Hence the phenomenon of personal forms of dependency coming to the fore by way of the suspension of valorisation with fictitious capital does not mean that abstract forms of domination are not also present.[11]

It may appear that the power dynamic implicit in fictitious capital is not a straightforward dichotomy between agents: while personal domination

11 Ibid.

by definition occurs at the level of direct inter-
action, debtors are mainly not individuals but
banks and hedge funds that speculate on future
production. And, in effect, are not the operations
of fictitious capital made more and more even
without *any* direct intervention, that is, simply
through computers that act on their programs?
However, these operations have to be somehow
retranslated into personal relations, and *there*
abstraction appears as personal domination.

Those who are not subjected to direct commodification but play a crucial role in the
reproduction of labour force are also affected by
the growing dependence on the future valorization that is supposed to be opened up by the
circulation of fictitious capital: fictitious capital
is upheld in the expectation that valorization
will occur in the future. Thus the reproduction
of labour power is put under pressure so that
those not labouring in the present will be ready to
labour in the future. This is why the topic of education (in its productive–technocratic version:
getting ready for the competitive job market) is
so important today, and is also intertwined with
debt: a student gets indebted in order to pay for
his or her education, and this debt is expected

to be repaid through self-commodification, that is, when the indebted student will get a job. Education also emerges as one of the main topics in discussions on how to deal with refugees – how to make them into a useful work force.

Since in our society free choice is elevated into a supreme value, social control and domination cannot be allowed to appear as infringing on the subject's freedom; they have to appear as, and be sustained by, the individuals' very experience of themselves as free. There is a multitude of forms in which this unfreedom appears in the guise of its opposite: when we are deprived of universal healthcare, we are told that we are given a new freedom of choice, namely to choose our healthcare provider; when we can no longer rely on long-term employment and are compelled to search for a new precarious position every couple of years, we are told that we are given the opportunity to reinvent ourselves and discover new, unexpected creative potentials that lurked in our personality; when we have to pay for the education of our children, we are told that we become 'entrepreneurs of the self', acting like a capitalist who has to choose freely how to invest the resources he or she possesses (or borrows) – into education, health, travel… Constantly bombarded by imposed 'free choices', forced to make decisions that we are, for the most part, not even properly qualified for (or do not possess enough information about), we increasingly experience our freedom as what it effectively is: a burden that deprives us of the true choice of change. Bourgeois society generally obliterates castes and other hierarchies, equalizing all individuals as market subjects divided only by class difference; but today's late capitalism, with its 'spontaneous' ideology, endeavours to obliterate the class division itself, by way of proclaiming us all 'self-entrepreneurs', the differences among us being merely quantitative (a big capitalist borrows hundreds of millions for his or her investment, a poor worker borrows a couple of thousands for his or her supplementary education). The expected outcome is that other divisions and hierarchies emerge: experts and nonexperts, full citizens and the excluded, religious, sexual, and other minorities. All the groups not yet included into the process of valorization, up to refugees and citizens of rogue countries, are thus progressively subsumed to forms of personal domination, from the organization of refugee camps to judicial control of those considered potential lawbreakers – a domination that tends to adopt a human face (as do social services intended to ease the refugees' smooth 'integration' into our societies).

The limits of Verwertung

All these complications compel us to rethink the so-called 'labour theory of value' – which should in no way be read as claiming that one should discard exchange, or its role in the constitution of value, as a mere appearance that obscures the key fact that labour is the origin of value. One should rather conceive of the emergence of value as a process of mediation by means of which value 'casts off' its use – value *is* surplus value over use value. The general equivalent of use values *had* to be deprived of use value, it had to function as a pure potentiality of use value. Essence is appearance as appearance: value is exchange value *as* exchange value – or, as Marx put it in a manuscript version of the changes to the first edition of *Capital*:

> The reduction of different concrete private labours to this abstraction [*Abstraktum*] of the same human

labour is accomplished only through exchange which effectively posits the products of different labours as equal to each other.[12]

In other words, 'abstract labour' is a value relationship that constitutes itself only in exchange, it is not the substantial property of a commodity independently of its relations with other commodities. For orthodox Marxists, such a relational notion of value is already a compromise with bourgeois political economy, which they dismiss as a monetary theory of value. However, the paradox is that these orthodox Marxists themselves effectively regress to the bourgeois notion of value: they conceive of value as being immanent in the commodity, as its property, and thus naturalize its spectral objectivity, which is the fetishized appearance of its social character.

We are not dealing here with mere theoretical niceties; the precise determination of the status of money has crucial economic–political consequences. If we consider money as a secondary form of expression of value that exists 'in itself' in a commodity before its expression – that is,

12 *Marx-Engels-Gesamtausgabe* [*MEGA*], Part II, vol. 6. Berlin: Dietz Verlag 1976, p. 41.

if money is for us a mere secondary resource, a practical means that facilitates exchange – then the door is open to the illusion, succumbed into by left-wing followers of Ricardo, that it would be possible to replace money with simple notes that designate the amount of work done by their bearer and give him or her the right to the corresponding part of the social product – as if, by means of this direct 'work money', one could avoid all 'fetishism' and ensure that each worker is paid his or her 'full value'. The point of Marx's analysis is that this project ignores the formal determinations of money that make fetishism a necessary effect. In other words, when Marx defines exchange value as the mode of appearance of value, one should mobilize here the entire Hegelian weight of the opposition between essence and appearance: essence exists only insofar as it appears, it does not preexist its appearance. In the same way, the value of a commodity is not an intrinsic substantial property that exists independently of that commodity's appearance in exchange.

This is also why we should abandon the attempts to expand value so that all kinds of labour will be recognized as a source of value. Recall the great feminist demand, in the 1970s, to legalize all housework, from cooking and household maintenance to looking after the children, as productive of value; or contemporary eco-capitalist demands to integrate the 'free gifts of nature' into value production by way of trying to determine the costs of water, air, forests, and all other commons. All these proposals are nothing but green-washing and commodification of a space from which a fierce attack upon the hegemony of the capitalist mode of production and its alienated relation to nature can be mounted. In their desire to be just and eliminate, or at least constrain, exploitation, such attempts only enforce an even stronger, all-encompassing commodification. Although they try to be just at the level of content, that is, about what counts as value, they fail to problematize the very *form* of commodification; and Harvey is right to propose instead to treat value as being in dialectical tension with nonvalue, in other words to assert and expand spheres not caught in the production of (market) value, such as household work or 'free' cultural and scientific work, in their crucial role. Value production can only thrive if it incorporates its immanent negation, the creative work that generates no (market) value, because the former is by definition parasitic on the latter. So, instead of commodifying exceptions and including them in the process of valorization, one should leave them outside and destroy the frame that makes their status inferior with regard to valorization. The problem with fictitious capital is not that it is outside valorization but that it remains parasitic on the fiction of a valorization to come.

A further challenge to market economy comes from the exploding virtualization of money, which compels us to reformulate thoroughly the standard Marxist topic of 'reification' and 'commodity fetishism', insofar as this topic still relies on the notion of fetish as a solid object whose stable presence obfuscates its social mediation. Paradoxically, fetishism reaches its acme precisely when the fetish itself is dematerialized, turned into a fluid, immaterial, virtual entity. Money fetishism will culminate in the transition to an electronic form of money, when the last traces of the materiality of money will disappear; electronic money is the third form, after 'real' money, which embodies its value directly (gold, silver), and paper money, which, although a mere sign with no intrinsic value, still clings to its material existence. And it is only at this stage, when money becomes a purely virtual point of reference, that it finally assumes the form of an indestructible spectral presence: I owe you £1,000 and, no matter how many material notes I burn, I still owe you £1,000 – the debt is inscribed somewhere in the virtual digital space... It is only with this thorough dematerialization – when Marx's famous old thesis in *The Communist Manifesto* that in capitalism 'all that is solid melts into air' acquires a much more literal meaning than the one he had in mind; when our material social reality is not only dominated by the spectral–speculative movement of capital but is itself progressively 'spectralized' (a 'Protean self' replaces the old self-identical subject, the elusive fluidity of its experiences replaces the stability of owned objects); in short, when the familiar relationship between firm material objects and fluid ideas is turned on its head (objects progressively dissolve into fluid experiences, while the only stable things are virtual symbolic obligations) – it is only at this point that what Derrida called the spectral aspect of capitalism is fully actualized.

However, as is always the case in a properly dialectical process, such a spectralization of the fetish contains the seeds of its opposite, of its self-negation: the unexpected return of direct relations of personal domination. While capitalism legitimizes itself as the economic system that implies and furthers personal freedoms (as a condition of market exchange), its own dynamics brought about a renaissance of slavery. Although slavery had become almost extinct at the end of the Middle Ages, it exploded again in the European colonies from early modernity until the American Civil War. And one can risk the hypothesis that today, in the new epoch of global capitalism, a new era of slavery is also arising. Although it no longer affects the direct legal status of enslaved persons, slavery acquires a multitude of new forms: millions of immigrant workers in the Saudi peninsula who are deprived of elementary civil rights and freedoms; total control over millions of workers in Asian sweatshops, which are often organized as concentration camps; massive use of forced labour in the exploitation of natural resources in many central African states (Congo and others). But in fact we don't have to look so far as these countries. On 1 December 2013, a Chinese-owned clothing factory in an industrial zone in the Italian town of Prato, 10 kilometres from the centre of Florence, burned down killing seven workers who were trapped inside, living and working in conditions of near slavery. So we cannot permit ourselves the luxury of looking at the miserable life of new slaves far away in the suburbs of Shanghai (or Dubai and Qatar) and hypocritically criticizing the countries that house them. Slavery can be right here, in our own house, we just don't see it – or rather we pretend not to see it. This new apartheid, this systematic explosion in the number of different forms of *de facto* slavery, is not a deplorable accident but a structural necessity of today's global capitalism.

Unfreedom in the guise of freedom

The Communist Manifesto is at its most actual when it enumerates different forms of false socialism. If what goes on in China today can be characterized as 'capitalist socialism', what, then, can we do with fundamentalist movements like Boko Haram? From the perspective of a traditional communal life, women's education is a key moment that encapsulates the devastating effect of western modernization; it 'liberates' women from family ties and trains them to become a part of the third world's cheap labour force. The struggle against women's education is thus a new form of what Marx and Engels, in *The Communist Manifesto*, called 'reactionary (feudal) socialism'. It signifies the rejection of the capitalist modernity in favour of traditional forms of communal life.

Another pertinent aspect of *The Communist Manifesto* is the series of answers it gives to the bourgeois reproach to communists ('You want to abolish property! You want to abolish marriage!'), which followed a precise Hegelian logic of dialectical *reversal*. *The Communist Manifesto* should be read here in parallel with the work of two other German artists from the same period: Heinrich Heine, from whom Marx and Engels borrowed many stylistic turns, and Richard Wagner, who was going through his early revolutionary period at the time (1848). The same insight was already formulated by Heinrich Heine in 1834, in his *History of Religion and Philosophy in Germany*, although presented there as a positive, admirable fact: 'Mark you this, you proud men of action, you are nothing but the unconscious henchmen of intellectuals, who, often in the humblest seclusion, have meticulously plotted your every deed.'[13] As cultural conservatives would have put it today, deconstructionist philosophers are much more dangerous than actual terrorists: while the latter want to undermine our politico-ethical order so as to impose their own religious-ethical order, deconstructionists want to undermine order itself, order qua order:

We say that the most dangerous criminal now is the entirely lawless modern philosopher. Compared to him, burglars and bigamists are essentially moral men; my heart goes out to them. They accept the essential ideal of man; they merely seek it wrongly. Thieves respect property. They merely wish the property to become their property that they may more perfectly respect it. But philosophers dislike property as property; they wish to destroy the very idea of personal possession. Bigamists respect marriage, or they would not go through the highly ceremonial and even ritualistic formality of bigamy. But philosophers despise marriage as marriage. Murderers respect human life; they merely wish to attain a greater fullness of human

13 Quoted from Dan Hind, *The Threat to Reason*. London: Verso Books 2007, p. 1.

39

life in themselves by the sacrifice of what seems to them to be lesser lives. But philosophers hate life itself, their own as much as other people's. ... The common criminal is a bad man, but at least he is, as it were, a conditional good man. He says that if only a certain obstacle be removed – say a wealthy uncle – he is then prepared to accept the universe and to praise God. He is a reformer, but not an anarchist. He wishes to cleanse the edifice, but not to destroy it. But the evil philosopher is not trying to alter things, but to annihilate them.[14]

This provocative analysis demonstrates the limitation of Chesterton, his not being Hegelian enough: what he doesn't get is that *universal(ized) crime is no longer a crime – it sublates (negates or overcomes) itself as crime and turns from transgression into a new order.* He is right to claim that, by comparison to the 'entirely lawless' philosopher, burglars, bigamists, murderers even are essentially moral: a thief is a conditionally good person, he or she doesn't deny property *qua property*, just wants more of it for him- or herself and is then

14 G.K. Chesterton, *The Man Who Was Thursday.* Harmondsworth: Penguin Books 1986, pp. 45–6.

quite ready to respect it. However, the conclusion to be drawn from this is that *crime is, qua crime, essentially moral*, that it wants just a particular, illegal reordering of a global moral order, while order itself should remain. And, in a truly Hegelian spirit, one should bring this proposition of the 'essential morality' of the crime to its immanent reversal. Not only is crime 'essentially moral' – in Hegelese: an inherent moment in the deployment of the inner antagonisms and contradictions of the very notion of moral order, rather than something that disturbs moral order from outside, as an accidental intrusion – but *morality itself is essentially criminal* – again, not only in the sense that the universal moral order necessarily 'negates itself' in particular crimes but, more radically, in the sense that *the way morality* (in the case of theft, property) *asserts itself is already in itself a crime*: 'property *is* theft', as they used to say in the nineteenth century. That is to say, one should pass from theft as a particular criminal violation of the universal form of property to this form itself as a criminal violation: what Chesterton fails to perceive is that the 'universalized crime' that he projects onto 'lawless modern philosophy' and its political equivalent, the 'anarchist' movement that aims at destroying the totality of civilized life, *already exists, in the guise of the current rule of law*, so that the antagonism between law and crime reveals itself to be inherent in crime, the antagonism between universal and particular crime. This point was clearly made by none other than Richard Wagner who, in his draft of the play *Jesus of Nazareth*, written somewhere between late 1848 and early 1849, attributes to Jesus a series of alternative supplementations of the Commandments:

> The commandment saith: Thou shalt not commit adultery! But I say unto you: Ye shall not marry without love. A marriage without love is broken as soon as entered into, and who so hath wooed without love, already hath broken the wedding. If ye follow my commandment, how can ye ever break it, since it bids you to do what your own heart and soul desire? – But where ye marry without love, ye bind yourselves at variance with God's love, and in your wedding ye sin against God; and this sin avengeth itself by your striving next against the law of man, in that ye break the marriage-vow.[15]

15 Richard Wagner, *Jesus of Nazareth and Other Writings*. Lincoln and London: University of Nebraska Press 1995, p. 303.

The shift from Jesus' actual words is crucial here. Jesus 'internalizes' the prohibition, rendering it much more severe (the law says no actual adultery, while I say that if you only covet the other's wife in your mind, it is the same as if you already committed adultery, etc.). Wagner also internalizes it, but in a different way: the inner dimension he evokes is not that of intention to do it, but that of love that should accompany the law (marriage). True adultery is not to copulate outside marriage but to copulate, in marriage, without love. Simple adultery just violates the law from outside, while a marriage without love destroys it from within, turning the letter of the law against its spirit. So, to paraphrase Brecht yet again, what is a simple adultery compared to (the adultery that is a loveless) marriage! It is not by chance that Wagner's underlying formula 'marriage is adultery' recalls Proudhon's 'property is theft'. In the stormy events of 1848, Wagner was not only a Feuerbachian celebrating sexual love, but also a Proudhonian revolutionary demanding the abolition of private property; so no wonder that, later on on the same page, Wagner attributes to Jesus a Proudhonian supplement to 'Thou shalt not steal!':

This also is a good law: Thou shalt not steal, nor covet another man's goods. Who goeth against it, sinneth: but I preserve you from that sin, inasmuch as I teach you: Love thy neighbour as thyself; which also meaneth: Lay not up for thyself treasures, whereby thou stealest from thy neighbour and makest him to starve: for when thou hast thy goods safeguarded by the law of man, thou provokest thy neighbour to sin against the law.[16]

This is how the Christian 'supplement' to the Book should be conceived of: as a properly Hegelian negation of negation, which resides in the decisive shift from the *distortion of a notion* to the *distortion that is constitutive of this notion* – that is, to this notion as a distortion in itself. Recall again Proudhon's old dialectical motto 'property is theft': the negation of negation is here the shift from theft as a distortion (negation, violation) of property to the dimension of theft as inscribed into the very notion of property. Nobody has the right to own means of production fully, since their nature is inherently collective; hence every claim of the form

16 Ibid., pp. 303–4.

'this is mine' is illegitimate. As we have just seen, the same goes for crime and law, for the transition from crime as a distortion (negation) of the law to crime as a sustainer of the law – in other words to the idea of law itself as universalized crime. One should note that, in this conception of Hegel's negation of negation, the unity encompassing the two opposite terms is the lowest, the transgressive one. It is not crime that represents a moment in law's self-mediation, and it is not theft that represents a moment in property's self-mediation; the opposition between crime and law is inherent in crime, hence law is a subspecies of crime, crime's self-relating negation, in the same way in which property is theft's self-relating negation. And does not the same hold, ultimately, of nature itself? Here negation of negation is the shift from the idea that we are violating some naturally balanced order to the idea that imposing on the real such a notion of balanced order is in itself the greatest violation... which is why the premise – or even the first axiom – of every radical ecology is that there is no nature. Chesterton wrote: 'Take away the supernatural and what you are left with is the unnatural.'[17] We should endorse this statement, but in the opposite sense from the one intended by Chesterton: we should accept that nature is 'unnatural', a freaky show of contingent disturbances with no inner rhyme. The same dialectical reversal characterizes the notion of violence. It is not only that violence (in the form of violent outbursts) is often an impotent *passage à l'acte*, a sign of impotence; one could claim that this reversal into impotence is not just the sign of a deficient violence but a feature inherent in violence itself: violence *qua violence* – the need to attack the opponent violently – is a sign of impotence, of the agent's exclusion from what it attacks. I only treat with violence things that escape my control, things that I cannot regulate and steer from within.

The two quotations from Wagner's play cannot but evoke the famous passages from *The Communist Manifesto* that answer the bourgeois reproach that communists want to abolish freedom, property, and family. Capitalist freedom is,

17 G.K. Chesterton, *Collected Works*, vol 1: *Heretics, Orthodoxies, the Blatchford Controversies*. San Francisco: Ignatius Press, 1986, p. 88.

in effect, the kind of freedom that one can buy and sell on the market, hence it is this freedom that represents the very form of unfreedom for those who have nothing but their labour force to sell. It is capitalist property itself that means 'abolition' of property for those who own no means of production. It is the bourgeois marriage itself that is a kind of universalized prostitution... In all these cases, the external opposition is internalized, so that one opposite becomes the form of appearance of the other: bourgeois freedom is the form of appearance of the unfreedom of the majority, and so on. But does not exactly the same hold for today's precarious 'self-entrepreneurs'? Their unfreedom – a precarious existence with no social welfare – appears to them in the guise of its opposite, as freedom to renegotiate the terms of one's existence many times over.

It is already a commonplace that the exploding rise of precarious work deeply affects the conditions of collective solidarity. Precarious work deprives workers of a whole series of rights that, until recently, were taken to be self-evident in any country that perceived itself as a welfare state. Workers themselves have to take care of their health insurance and retirement options; there is no paid leave; and the future is uncertain. Besides, precarious work generates antagonism within the working class, between permanently employed and precarious workers; trade unions often tend to privilege permanent workers and it is very difficult for precarious workers even to organize themselves into a union or to establish another form of collective self-organization. One might have expected that this strengthened exploitation would also strengthen workers' resistance, but in fact it renders resistance even more difficult. The main reason for this is ideological. Precarious work is presented (and up to a point even effectively experienced) as a new form of freedom: I am no longer just a cog in a complex enterprise but an entrepreneur of the self, I am my own boss – someone who freely manages his or her employment, is free to choose from new options, to explore different aspects of his or her creative potential, to decide his or her priorities...

The communist horizon

So, to conclude, the vision that underlies *The Communist Manifesto* is that of a society gradually approaching its final crisis, a situation in which the complexity of social life is simplified into one great antagonism between capitalists and the proletarian majority. However, even a quick look at the twentieth-century communist revolutions makes it clear that this simplification never took place: radical communist movements were always confined to a minority in the vanguard and, in order for it to gain hegemony, it had to wait patiently for a crisis – usually a war – to provide a narrow window of opportunity. Those are the moments when an authentic vanguard can seize the day, mobilize the people, even if not an actual majority, and take over. Communists were always utterly nondogmatic in this respect, ready to parasitize other issues – be they land and peace, as in Russia, or national liberation and unity against corruption, as in China... They were always well aware that mobilization will be soon over, and were carefully preparing the power apparatus to keep them in power at that moment. (In contrast to the October Revolution, which explicitly treated peasants as secondary allies, the Chinese revolution didn't even pretend to be proletarian: it directly addressed farmers as its base.)

The problem of western Marxism (and even of Marxism *tout court*) was the absence of the revolutionary subject: how is it that the working class did not complete the passage from being 'in itself' to being 'for itself' and did not constitute itself as a revolutionary agent? This problem provided the main reason for its appeal to psychoanalysis, which was evoked precisely to explain the unconscious libidinal mechanisms that prevent the rise of a class consciousness inscribed in the very being (or social condition) of the working class. In this way the truth of Marxist socioeconomic analysis was saved and there was no reason to give ground to revisionist theories about the rise of the middle classes. For the same reason, western Marxism was also in a constant search for other social groups that could play the role of the revolutionary agent, be the understudy ready to replace the indisposed working class: third-world peasants, students, and intellectuals, the excluded marginals… The latest version of this idea operates with refugees: only the influx of a really large number of refugees can revitalize the European radical left. This line of thought is thoroughly obscene and cynical: notwithstanding the fact that such a development would, for sure, give an immense boost to anti-immigrant brutality, the truly crazy aspect of this idea is the project of filling in the gap left by absent proletarians by importing stand-ins from abroad. This way one gets a revolution outsourced from a surrogate revolutionary agent.

The failure of the working class as revolutionary subject lay already at the core of the Bolshevik revolution. Lenin's art was to detect the 'potential for rage' (to adopt Sloterdijk's concept) of the disappointed peasants. The October Revolution won thanks to the slogan 'land and peace', addressed to the vast majority of peasants and well calculated to seize the short moment of their radical dissatisfaction. At the time of the 1918 Revolution Lenin had been thinking along these lines for a decade or so, which is why he was horrified at the prospect of the success of the Stolypin land reforms, which aimed at creating a new, strong class of independent farmers; he wrote that, if Stolypin succeeds, the chance for a revolution is lost for decades. All successful socialist revolutions, from Cuba to Yugoslavia, followed this model, seizing their chances in an extreme critical situation and co-opting the cause of national liberation or other forms of 'rage capital'. Of course, a partisan of the logic of hegemony would point out here that this is a very 'normal' logic of revolutions and that critical mass is reached precisely and only through a series of equivalences among multiple demands – a fact that is always radically contingent and that depends on a specific, even unique set of circumstances. A revolution never occurs when all antagonisms collapse into the big One, but when they synergetically combine their power.

The problem here is rather complex. The point is not just that revolution no longer rides the train of history in accordance with its laws – since there is no history, since history is a contingent and open process; there is a different problem. It is as if there *is* a law of history, a more or less clear and predominant main line of historical development, which indicates that revolution can occur only in interstices, against the current. Revolutionaries have to wait patiently for the (usually very brief) period of time when the system openly malfunctions or collapses, seize their window of opportunity, grab the power – which at that moment lies in the street and is up for grabs, as it were – and then fortify their hold on it by building repressive apparatuses and what not, so that, once the moment of confusion is over and the majority gets sober and disappointed by the new regime, it is too late to get rid of them, they are firmly entrenched. Communists were also always carefully calculating the right moment to stop popular mobilization. Let's take the case of the Chinese Cultural Revolution, which undoubtedly contained the elements of an enacted utopia. At its very end, before the agitation was blocked by Mao himself – since he had already achieved his goals of regaining full power and getting rid of competition in the top ranks of the *nomenklatura* – there was the Shanghai Commune: 1 million workers who simply took the official slogans seriously, demanding the abolition of the state, even of the party itself, and a direct, communal organization of society. It is significant that it was at this very point that Mao ordered the army to intervene and to restore order. The paradox is that of a leader who triggers an uncontrolled upheaval while trying to exert full personal power, in an overlap between extreme dictatorship and extreme emancipation of the masses.

In a short poem written apropos the German Democratic Republic (GDR) workers' uprising in 1953, Brecht quotes a contemporary party functionary as saying that 'the people' has lost the government's trust: would it not therefore be easier, Brecht slyly asks, to dissolve this people and have the government elect another one? Instead of reading this poem as a case of Brechtian irony, one should take it seriously: yes, in a situation of popular mobilization, 'the people' is in a way replaced, transubstantiated (the inert mass of ordinary people is transubstantiated into a politically engaged united force). The problem is, again, that this transubstantiation cannot last forever; one should always bear in mind that a permanent presence of the people equals a permanent state of exception. So what happens when 'the people' gets tired, when people are no longer able to sustain the tension? Communists in power had two solutions (or rather two sides of one and the same solution): the party's reign over a passive population; and a fake popular mobilization. Trotsky himself, the theorist of 'permanent revolution', was well aware that people 'cannot live for years in an uninterrupted state of high tension and intense activity'[18] and turned this fact into an

18 Ernest Mandel, *Trotsky as Alternative*. London: Verso Books 1995, p. 81.

argument about the need for a vanguard party: self-organization into councils cannot take over the role of the party, which should run things when people get tired... and, to amuse them and maintain appearances, an occasional big spectacle of pseudo-mobilization has proved to be of some use, from Stalinist parades to North Korea's massive military displays today. In capitalist countries there is, of course, another way to dispel popular pressure: (more or less) free elections – recently in Egypt and Turkey, but in 1968 they worked in France, too. One should not forget that the agent of popular pressure is always a minority – even the Occupy Wall Street was, with regard to its active participants, much closer to 1 per cent than to the 99 per cent of its big slogan.

The underlying problem here is the one I already encountered at the beginning of my essay. How are we to think of the singular universality of the emancipatory subject as not purely formal, that is, as objectively, materially determined, yet without the working class as its substantial base? The solution is a negative one: it is capitalism itself that offers a negative substantive determination. The global capitalist system is the substantive 'base' that mediates and generates the excesses (slums, ecological threats, etc.) that open up the site of resistance. Left-wing visions abound around us of how our task is to bring together different groups of the exploited and underprivileged of today's global capitalism (immigrants, unemployed, pre-carious workers, victims of sexual, racial, and religious oppression, dissatisfied students...) into a united front of emancipatory struggle; but the problem is that we, in clear contrast to Marxists, can no longer envisage the process of this unifica-tion in global solidarity.

The question of the continuing relevance of Marx's critique of political economy in our era of global capitalism has to be answered in a properly dialectical way: not only are Marx's critique of political economy and his outline of capitalist dynamics still fully actual, one should take one step further and claim that it is only today, with global capitalism, that, to put it in Hegelese, reality arrived at these notions. However, a properly dialectical reversal inter-venes here: at this very moment of full actuality, the limitation has to appear; the moment of triumph is that of defeat; after the overcom-ing of external obstacles, the new threat comes from within, signalling an immanent inconsistency. When reality fully reaches up to its notion, this notion itself has to be transformed. Therein resides the properly dialectical paradox: Marx was not simply wrong, he was often right, but more literally than he himself expected to be.

So what is the conclusion? Should we write off *The Communist Manifesto* as an interesting document of the past and nothing more? In a properly dialectical paradox, the very impasses and failures of twentieth-century communism, impasses that were clearly grounded in the limitations of *The Communist Manifesto* itself, at the same time bear witness to its actuality: the classic Marxist solution failed, but the problem remains. Today communism is not the name of a solution but the name of a *problem*, namely that of *commons* in all its dimensions: the problem of a commons of nature as the substance of our life, the problem of our biogenetic commons, the problem of our cultural commons ('intellectual property'), and, last but not least, the problem of a commons as the universal space of humanity from which no one should be excluded. Whatever the solution, it will have to deal with *these* problems.

In Soviet translations, Marx's well-known statement to Paul Lafargue, *Ce qu'il y a de certain, c'est que moi je ne suis pas marxiste* ['What is certain is that I am not a Marxist'], was rendered thus: 'If this is Marxism then I am not a Marxist.' This mistranslation renders perfectly the transformation of Marxism in university discourse. In Soviet Marxism, even Marx was a Marxist and participated in the same universal knowledge that composes Marxism; the fact that he created the teaching later known by this label made no difference. So his denial above does not refer just to a specific, wrong version that falsely proclaimed itself to be 'Marxism'. Marx meant something more radical: a gap separates him, the creator who has a substantive relationship with his teaching, from the 'Marxists' who follow this teaching. There is a well-known joke by the Marx Brothers that captures this idea: 'You look like Emmanuel Ravelli. – But I am Emmanuel Ravelli. – So no wonder you look like him.' The guy who is Ravelli doesn't look like Ravelli, he simply is Ravelli. In the same way, Marx himself is not a Marxist – one among others; he is the point of reference exempted from the series, because it is by reference to him that others are

Marxists. And the only way to remain faithful to Marx today is to stop being a Marxist and to repeat instead Marx's grounding gesture in a new way.